What Was the Bo[illegible] Hiros[illegible]ma?

What Was the Bombing of Hiroshima?

by Jess Brallier

illustrated by Tim Foley

Penguin Workshop

For Family—JB

PENGUIN WORKSHOP
An Imprint of Penguin Random House LLC, New York

Published by Penguin Workshop, an imprint of Penguin Random House LLC, New York.
PENGUIN and PENGUIN WORKSHOP are trademarks of Penguin Books Ltd.
WHO HQ & Design is a registered trademark of Penguin Random House LLC.
Printed in the USA.

Visit us online at www.penguinrandomhouse.com.

Library of Congress Control Number: 2019034738

ISBN 9781524792657 (paperback)
ISBN 9781524792664 (library binding)

10 9 8 7 6 5 4 3 2
10 9 8 7 6 5 4 3 2 1

Contents

What Was the Bombing of Hiroshima? 1

Japan 5

World War II 14

The Manhattan Project 28

Decision Time 41

The Bombing of Hiroshima 48

Stories of Survivors 58

The War Ends 67

What Followed 84

The Peace Museum 93

Timelines 100

Bibliography 105

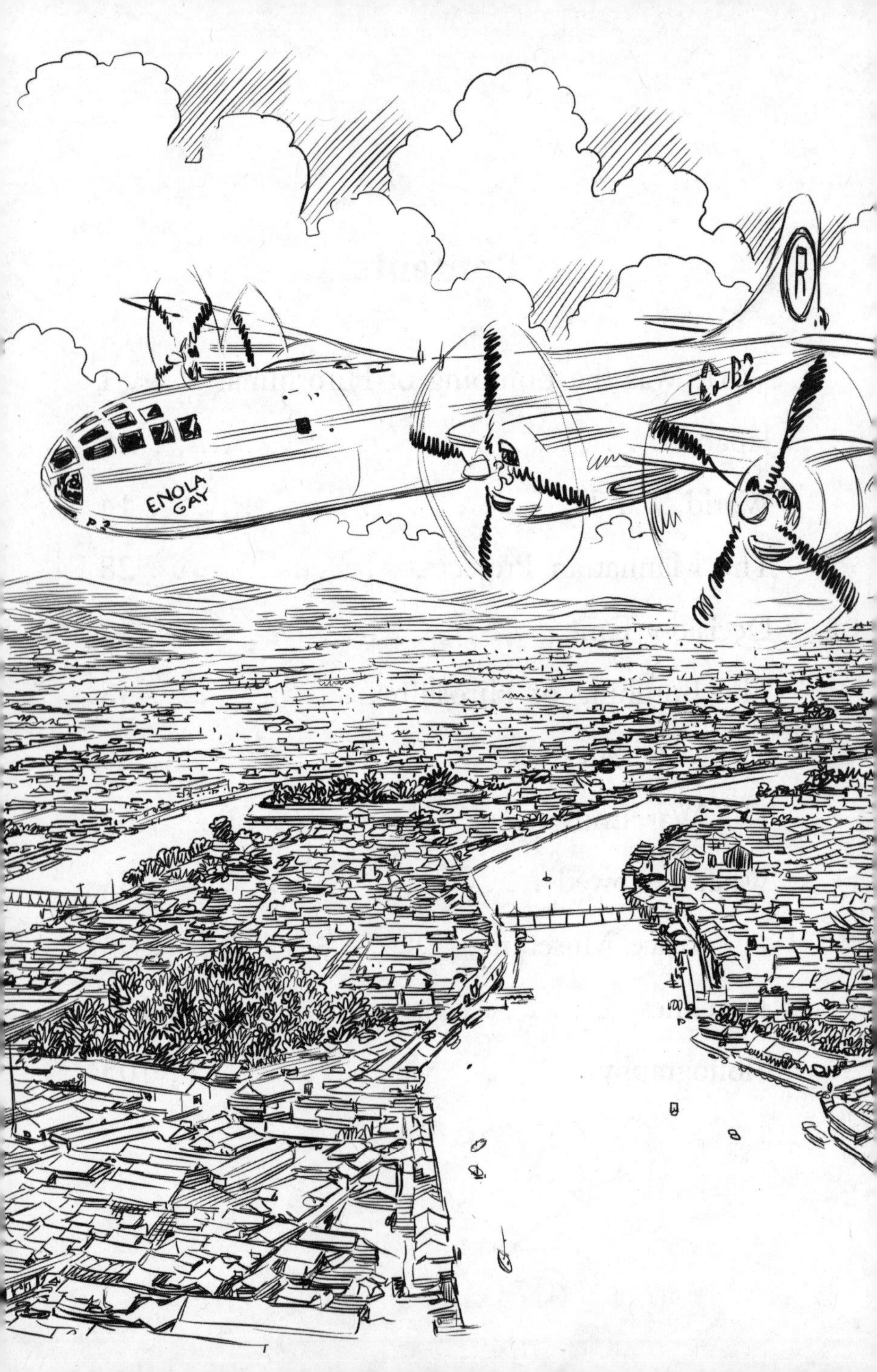
ENOLA
GAY
R

What Was the Bombing of Hiroshima?

In the early morning on August 6, 1945, an American B-29 bomber flew toward Japan. The plane was named the *Enola Gay* after the mother of its pilot, Colonel Paul Tibbets. In its cargo was a weapon unlike any the world had known.

As the bomber flew closer to its target, Tibbets revealed to his crew what the secret weapon was. Their plane was carrying the first atomic bomb that would ever be used in war.

The bomb was nicknamed "Little Boy." And it was going to be dropped on the Japanese city of Hiroshima.

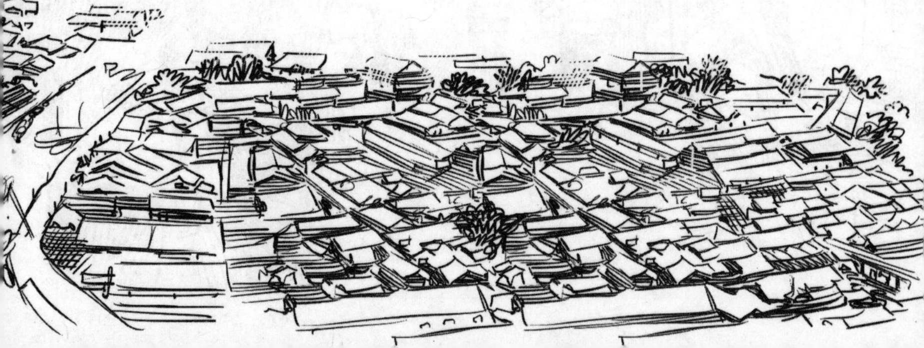

Below, the 350,000 citizens of Hiroshima were beginning their day. Eating breakfast, walking to school, reading a newspaper, arriving at work. They had no idea what was about to happen.

At 8:15, the *Enola Gay*'s bomb bay door opened, and Little Boy was dropped. Less than a minute later, the atomic bomb exploded.

Suddenly, for miles in all directions, fires ignited. Metal melted, and sixty thousand buildings were destroyed. About seventy thousand people died instantly or were fatally injured. Eventually, over two hundred thousand people would die from the bomb.

For the first time ever, an atomic weapon had been let loose. Its ability to kill and destroy was nearly beyond imagination. Who decided to drop it? And why? Was the decision right or wrong? That debate continues, even as you read this. What cannot be debated, however, is that on August 6, 1945, the world changed forever.

Bombs . . . and Atomic Bombs

Before the atomic bomb, both sides in the war had dropped many conventional bombs on cities. A conventional bomb releases energy from a chemical reaction. It causes major death and destruction. But after exploding, it does no further damage. An atomic bomb, however, releases radiation, and after it explodes, the radiation continues to kill people for decades. The explosive power of one small atomic bomb is more than 2,300 times as powerful as any conventional bomb ever used.

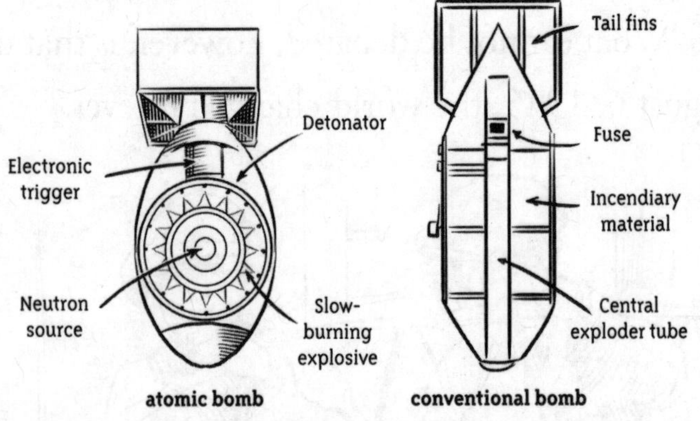

CHAPTER 1
Japan

Before the late 1800s, Japan had little contact with Europe or the Americas.

Emperors had controlled Japan from about 660 until the 1100s. Then military rulers, called shoguns, took over. The shoguns commanded samurai, who were noble soldiers similar to European knights. Ranked below the samurai were foot soldiers, called *ashigaru*.

Shogun

The samurai dressed in armor held together by silk cords. They followed a code of conduct known as Bushido, or "the way of the warrior." Samurai were to be honest, loyal, and above all, brave. No samurai could bear to live in dishonor. In the 1500s, European traders first sailed to Japan. They wanted to buy and sell goods with the Japanese. Shoguns, fearing change and loss of their own power, banned almost all outsiders in 1641.

Samurai

After that, Japan remained largely cut off from the Western world until 1853. That's when the US Navy commodore Matthew Perry sailed into Tokyo, Japan's biggest city. Commodore Perry forced the shoguns to allow trade with the United States.

Commodore Matthew Perry

Japan

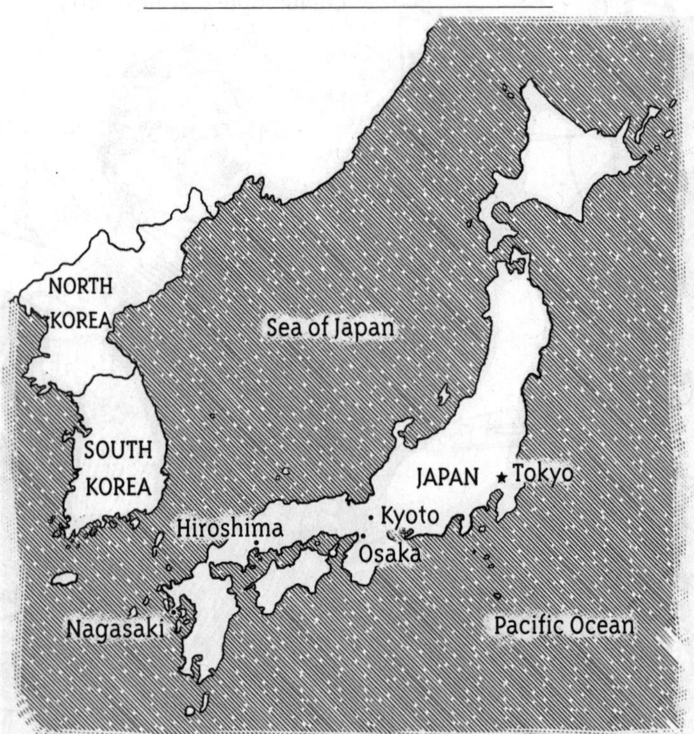

The nation of Japan comprises a string of islands along the eastern edge of Asia in the Pacific Ocean. In 1945, its population was 72 million. Today, it's over 126 million. A leader in various industries, Japan is the home of Nintendo and Pokémon.

From then on, the country began to blend Western ways with its own values. And emperors again replaced the shoguns. But the emperor also served as Japan's religious leader. His ministers controlled the government. Japan became a military power, and it set up big businesses, moving people from farms to factories. However, Japan lacked many natural resources, such as oil and rubber. It needed them to make many products. So Japan depended on buying these things from other nations.

Tokyo, Japan, in the 1920s

In the 1930s, Japan continued to grow in might. Meanwhile, the United States was going through the hard years of the Great Depression. Millions lost their jobs and homes. Poverty spread throughout the country. The United States elected Franklin D. Roosevelt as president in 1932. President Roosevelt promised people a New Deal. That meant that the government would start large programs to try to get people working again.

Franklin Delano Roosevelt (1882–1945)

Franklin Delano Roosevelt served as the thirty-second president of the United States from 1933 to 1945. He served longer than any other president.

Roosevelt suffered from the then common disease of polio. Unable to walk, he was confined to a wheelchair. That didn't stop him from being a strong leader. He was elected four times and died in office near the very end of World War II. In 1951, an amendment (change) was made to the US Constitution. After that, a president could be elected for no more than two four-year terms.

Countries in Europe were suffering through the Depression as well. In Germany, Italy, and Spain, people turned to dictators—rulers with total control—to solve their problems. There was Adolf Hitler in Germany, Benito Mussolini in Italy, and Francisco Franco in Spain. Hitler was the most powerful. His plan was to take over all of Europe.

The United States was against these dictators but hoped to stay out of Europe's problems. After all, many Americans said, Europe was far away, across an ocean. And the United States was not under attack.

But that soon would change.

Adolf Hitler

CHAPTER 2
World War II

In 1939, Adolf Hitler and his Nazi troops stormed into Poland and took over the country. In response, Great Britain and France declared war on Germany, and Italy sided with Hitler. This was the start of World War II.

The Nazis conquered one country after another. In 1940, Denmark, France, Norway, the Netherlands, Belgium, and Luxembourg fell. Great Britain was left alone to fight Hitler's forces.

President Roosevelt was willing to provide equipment—such as planes and weapons—to help the British. But he did not send American soldiers.

Japan saw Germany's success as its chance to attack parts of Asia, some of which were controlled by European powers. Japan had already begun a brutal invasion of China in 1937. In 1940, Japan invaded French Indochina (what today is Vietnam).

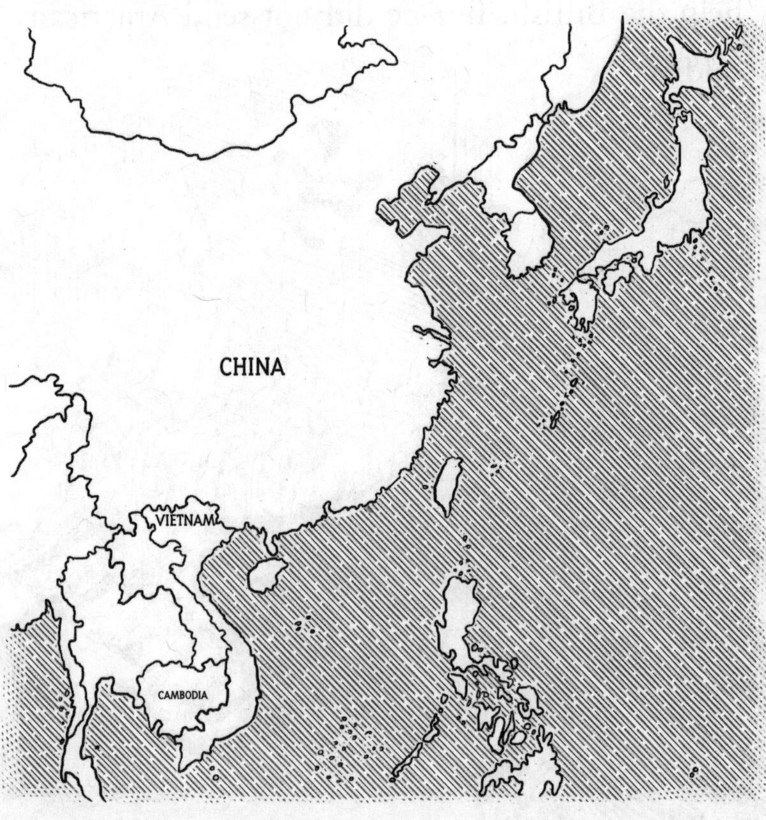

However, for its military goals, Japan needed lots of metal and oil. The problem was that these came from the United States. Americans did not like selling Japan these materials, knowing of its plans. Also, Japan and Nazi Germany had been allies since 1936. President Roosevelt soon banned the sale of metal and oil to Japan. This made the Japanese government really angry.

LATE CITY EDITION

The New York Times.

EMBARGO PUT ON OIL, SCRAP METAL IN LICENSE ORDER BY ROOSEVELT; FRENCH SHIP SUNK, 350 DROWNED

JOHNSON RESIGNS AS STIMSON AIDE; PATTERSON NAMED

WALLACE DEFERS 'POLITICAL' MOVES TILL HE IS NOTIFIED

JOB SAFEGUARD PUT INTO TRAINING BILL

LINER IS TORPEDOED

ARGENTINA BLOCKS TRUSTEESHIP PLAN

The International Situation

The Japanese military wanted to end American power in Asia once and for all. The United States knew this, and believed that an attack might come. In fact, it looked almost certain. But no one imagined where it would take place.

Pearl Harbor is in Hawaii. In 1941, Hawaii was part of the United States, but was not a US state yet. The United States had airfields, power plants, and nearly eighteen thousand

military personnel stationed at Pearl Harbor. Eight battleships were anchored together. They were lined up neatly, in what was called Battleship Row.

In the early morning of December 7, 1941, over 350 Japanese planes suddenly filled the skies above Pearl Harbor. Bombs fell. Nineteen US Navy ships were damaged or destroyed, and more than 2,400 Americans were killed.

The next day, the United States declared war on Japan.

Now America was part of World War II. Roosevelt sent troops to fight the Japanese in the Pacific as well as troops to Europe to help the British defeat the Germans.

Allies vs. Axis

World War II was fought between the Allies and the Axis Powers. The main Allied partners were Great Britain, France, the United States, and the Soviet Union. The Axis forces were led by Germany, Japan, and Italy. As the war continued, countries around the world began to join the opposing sides. Canada, Brazil, South Africa, China, and Australia—among others—joined the Allies. Some Eastern European nations joined the Axis powers.

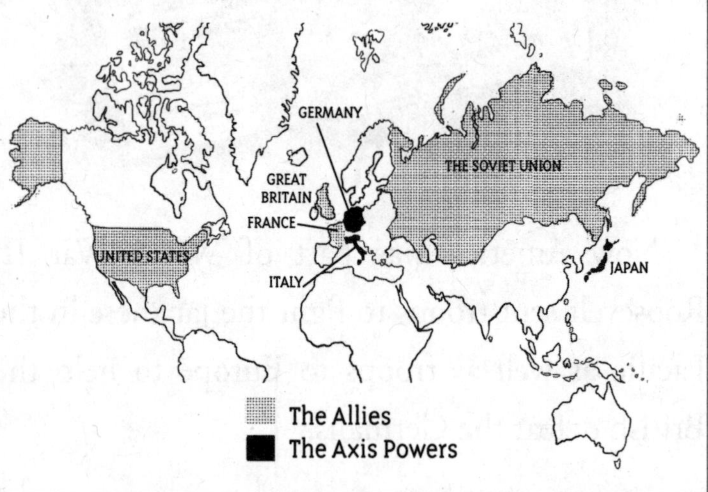

At first, Japan scored victories against the United States and its allies. It won attacks on Hong Kong, British Malaya, and the Philippines. In the Philippines, the United States suffered one of its worst defeats, at the Battle of Bataan. Seventy thousand American and Filipino soldiers had to surrender.

Japanese tanks ride through Bataan

Internment Camps (1942–1946)

Shortly after Japan's attack on Pearl Harbor, President Roosevelt ordered nearly 117,000 Japanese Americans to leave their homes and go to live in "camps." These men, women, and children were American citizens. Many families had sons serving in the US military. And yet they were put behind barbed wire and watched by armed officers in guard towers.

Journalist Michiko Kakutani wrote of her mother's family: "They were allowed to take only what they could carry. Everything else had to be sold, thrown out, given to friends or put in storage. . . . [My family was placed in] a horse stall, 10 feet by 20 feet, furnished with Army cots and still smelling of horse manure."

The camps were closed by early 1946. In 1988, the Civil Liberties Act, signed by President Ronald Reagan, admitted that its internment actions were based on "race prejudice, war hysteria, and a failure of political leadership." Every still-living survivor of an internment camp was also given $20,000.

By midsummer 1942, the tide of war turned. The Americans put Japan on the defensive. The Allies now advanced steadily toward Japan. Island after island in the Pacific was captured. Eventually Japan itself was within reach of US bombers.

In Europe, Italy surrendered to the Allies in 1943, and by 1945 Hitler's army was at the point of collapse. Major cities in Germany had been bombed. Destroying them helped ensure Allied victory.

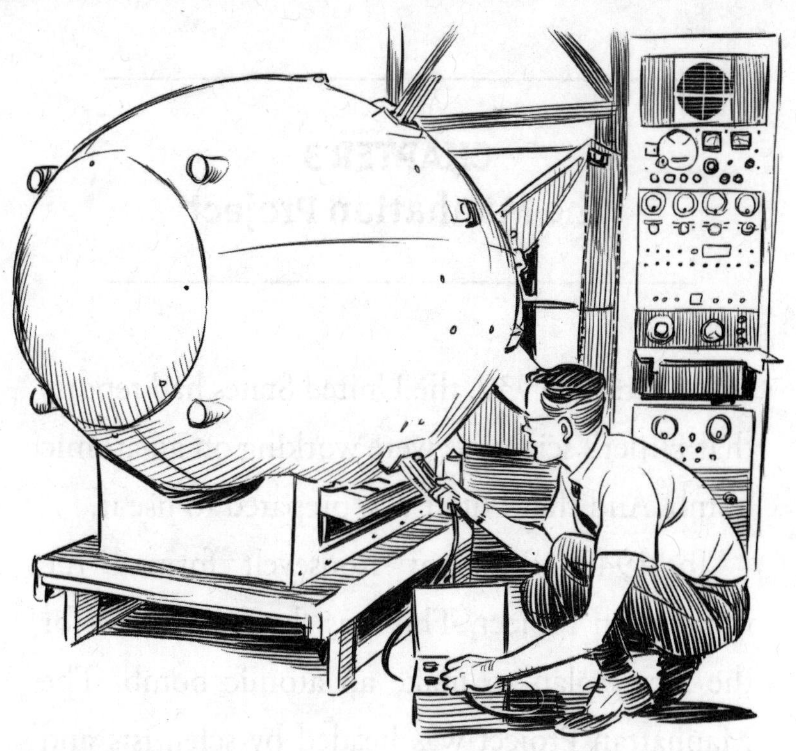

Would massive bombings destroying Japan's major cities end the war in the Pacific as well? Or would a new kind of weapon be needed to make Japan surrender? For years, Roosevelt had had a group of scientists working on a new kind of weapon. Something way more deadly than anything seen before.

An atomic bomb.

CHAPTER 3
The Manhattan Project

As early as 1939, the United States had reports that Hitler's scientists were working on an atomic bomb. And that Hitler was prepared to use it.

In 1942, President Roosevelt formed the Manhattan Project. This was the code name for the secret plan to make an atomic bomb. The Manhattan Project was headed by scientists and engineers, many of them Germans and Hungarians who had recently escaped from Europe.

The project was first based out of offices in Manhattan. New York City had much to offer. It had many physics laboratories, including one at Columbia University. (Columbia's football team was even used to move heavy supplies.) There were also three warehouses near the city's Hudson

River storing tons of uranium ore shipped from Africa. Uranium was a key ingredient in making an atomic bomb.

Schermerhorn Hall at Columbia University,
where research was conducted for the Manhattan Project

Albert Einstein (1879–1955)

The most famous scientist of the time was Albert Einstein. Einstein, who was Jewish, had moved to the United States in 1933. He was fleeing the Nazis, who hated all Jews. In 1939, he wrote to President Roosevelt. He warned that America's enemies were developing an atomic bomb. Einstein's letter helped convince Roosevelt to do the same.

After the war, however, Einstein worked with others to end nuclear weapons. He later said of his warning to President Roosevelt, "Had I known that the Germans would not succeed in producing an atomic bomb, I would not have lifted a finger."

However, a very crowded Manhattan did not provide the larger testing grounds needed. Manhattan was also not isolated enough for the project's required security.

Manhattan in the 1940s

Facilities were soon set up far away from New York, in Oak Ridge, Tennessee; Hanford, Washington; and Los Alamos, New Mexico. Yet the project's "Manhattan" name was kept. Physicist J. Robert Oppenheimer was put in charge of creating and heading the laboratory at Los Alamos. There the bomb would be assembled and tested.

J. Robert Oppenheimer

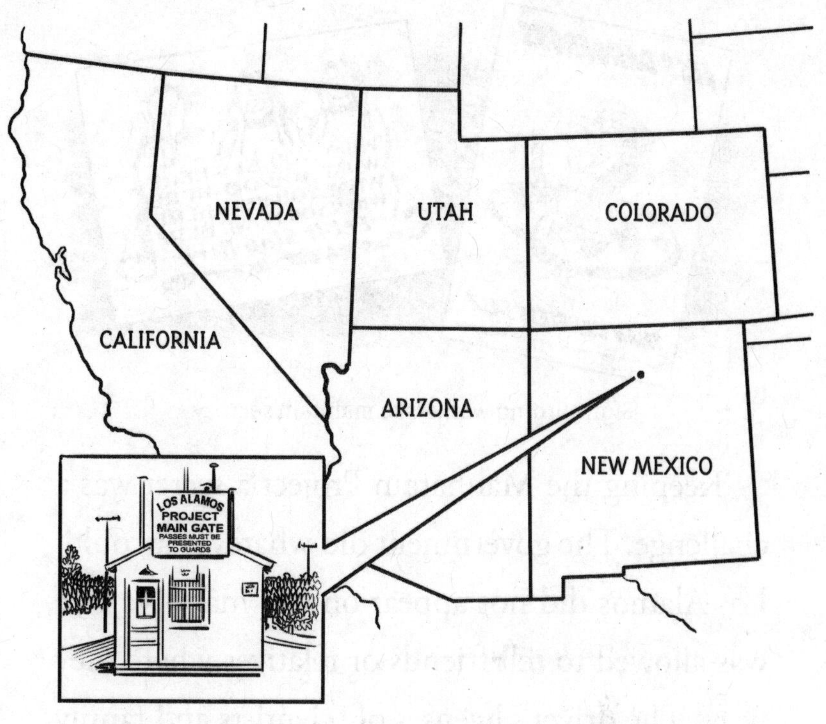

The Los Alamos base was constructed almost overnight on the grounds of a private school in the desert. Here many of the country's top scientists lived and worked in a guarded camp with their families. Surrounded by fences, the base had huge laboratory buildings on the south side, rows of apartments on the west side. A few boardwalks kept residents out of the mud when snow melted.

Signs urging workers to maintain secrecy

Keeping the Manhattan Project a secret was a challenge. The government did whatever it could. Los Alamos did not appear on any map. No one was allowed to tell friends or relatives where they were. The driver's licenses of scientists and family members had no names on them, only identifying numbers. Even magazine subscriptions were not allowed. Nobody's name could be on a mailing list.

By the end of the war, Los Alamos had a population of six thousand. Yet, a single post office box, P.O. Box 1663, served everybody. The birth certificates for babies born in the seven-room hospital had only "P.O. Box 1663" listed as their birthplace. The babies included Oppenheimer's daughter, Toni, born in December 1944.

Despite the strangeness, Los Alamos residents tried to have a normal life. There were schools, and also theaters, one of which served as a dance hall on Saturdays and a church on Sundays. Families took turns hosting parties in their homes.

At Los Alamos, scientists discovered how to make a powerful weapon by releasing the energy stored inside uranium atoms. (Everything in the universe is made of microscopic particles called atoms.)

At the center of an atom is its nucleus, which contains neutrons and protons. An extreme amount of energy holds neutrons and protons together inside the nucleus. Splitting an atom's nucleus releases that energy.

As a nucleus splits, neutrons shoot out. When a neutron hits another nucleus, that nucleus splits and shoots out more neutrons. Those in turn do the same. And so on and so on at a fast pace. With each step of the chain reaction, more energy is released. This splitting of nuclei process is called fission.

In nature, most atoms are not easily split. When a neutron strikes these elements, the chain reaction does not continue.

But uranium atoms split easily. In an atomic bomb, uranium atoms are concentrated, or grouped together tightly. An atomic bomb's violent explosive power is the sudden release of all that energy.

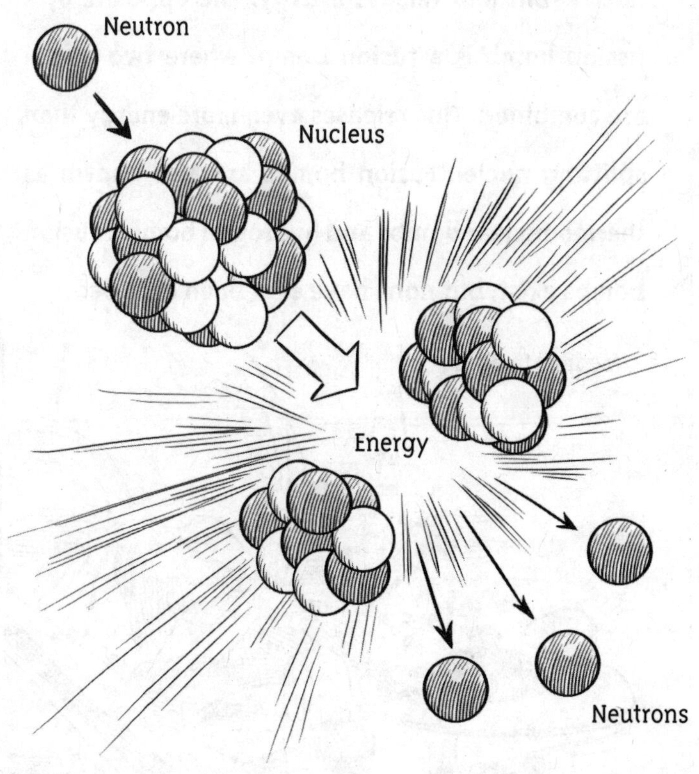

Nuclear fission process

Fission vs. Fusion

The atomic bombs dropped on both Hiroshima and Nagasaki were fission bombs. In a fission bomb, nuclei split and release energy. The opposite of a fission bomb is a fusion bomb, where two nuclei are combined. This releases even more energy than splitting nuclei. Fusion bombs are also known as thermonuclear bombs and hydrogen bombs. Fusion bombs exist, but none have ever been dropped.

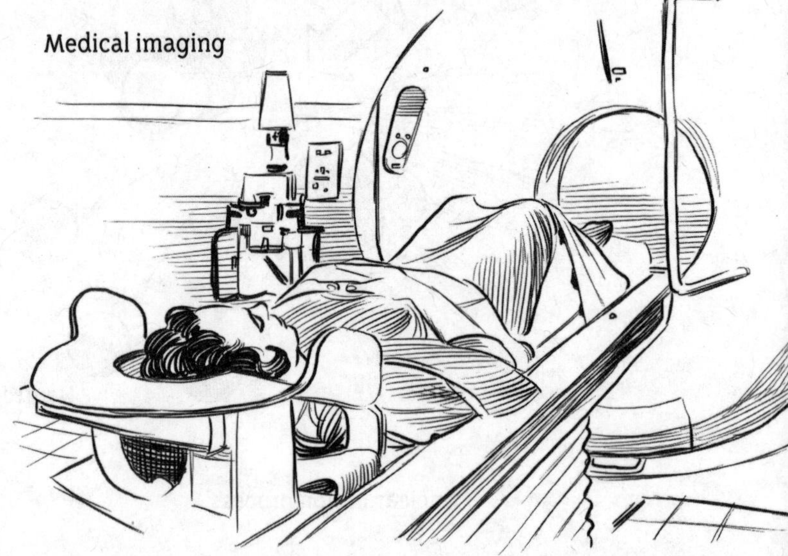

Medical imaging

The technology developed by the Manhattan Project is also used for nonmilitary purposes. These include medical imaging, radiation therapies for cancer, and, through nuclear power plants, the generation of energy for homes, schools, hospitals, factories, and other businesses. Many believe that nuclear power is a cleaner energy source than natural gas, coal, and oil, which are believed to harm our world and its climate.

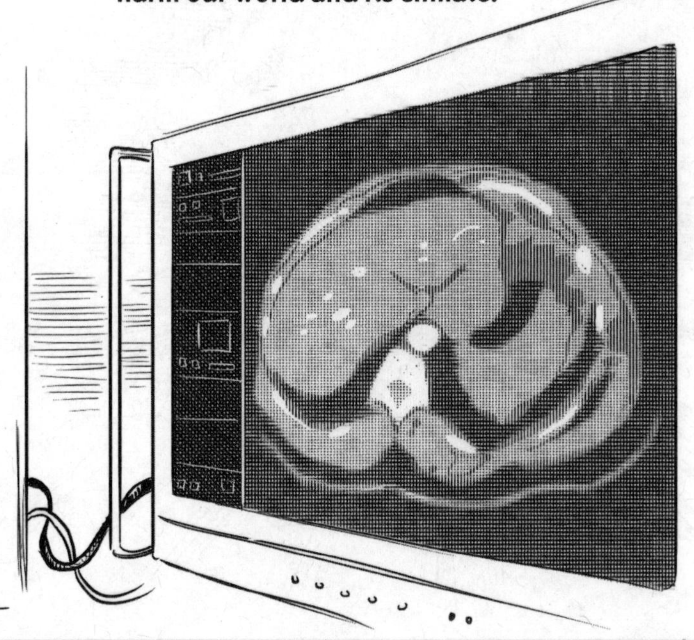

On July 16, 1945, the first atomic bomb was detonated (set off) as a test, in the New Mexico desert, where no people would be hurt. It created an enormous mushroom cloud almost eight miles high. Here was proof. The bomb worked!

CHAPTER 4
Decision Time

By the time the successful test in New Mexico occurred, Germany had surrendered. But not Japan. It wanted to fight to the bitter end. So, the United States had a decision to make. How was it going to defeat the enemy?

One way was to mount an all-out attack on Japan. The plan was code-named Operation Downfall. It would begin in November 1945.

First, smaller islands near Japan had to be captured. From those islands, it would be easier for US bomber planes to attack Japan.

Next, the southern third of Japan's main island would be invaded and captured. This required American soldiers to land on Japanese shores from warships.

Then, in the spring of 1946, the Allies would invade near Tokyo.

The United States knew that their troops would be met with everything Japan had. Up to one million American soldiers might die in Operation Downfall. (By the end of the war, 416,800 US soldiers, sailors, airmen, and marines had been killed. More than 670,000 were wounded in Europe and the Pacific.) Many Americans believed: *Enough is enough.*

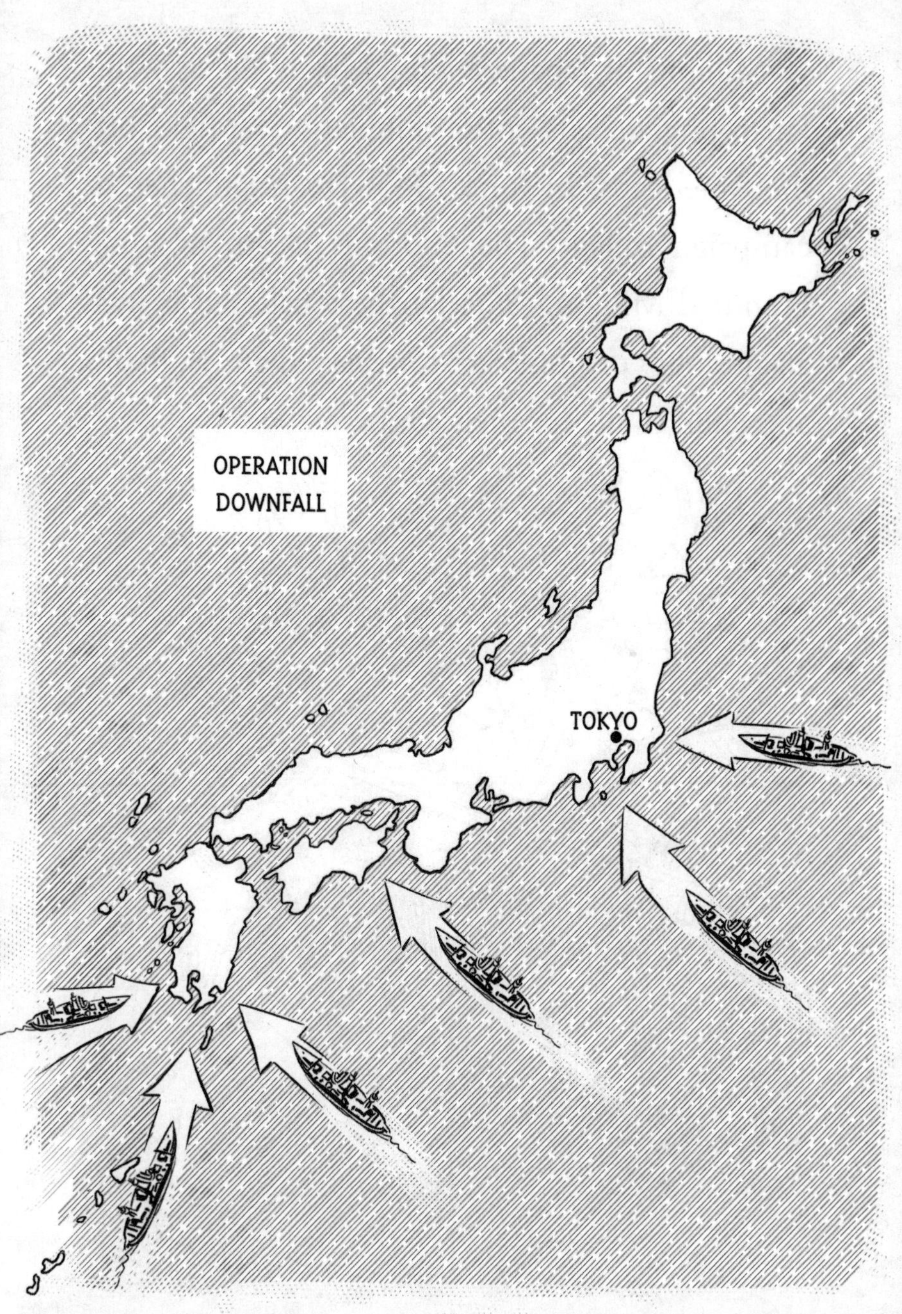
OPERATION
DOWNFALL
TOKYO

Millions of Japanese would likely die as well. Japan prepared its entire population to fight off the Americans. In June 1945, Japan launched a campaign called "The Glorious Death of One Hundred Million." The Japanese believed it was a "glorious" or noble act for every man, woman, and child to die for their country.

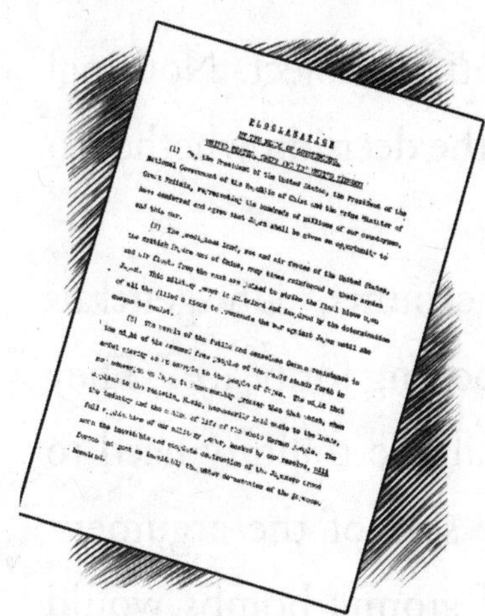

Terms for Japan's surrender known as the Potsdam Declaration

In July 1945, the United States wrote out terms for Japan's surrender. A surrender would avoid starting Operation Downfall or using the atomic bomb.

But Japan refused to give up.

The New York Times.

PRESIDENT ROOSEVELT IS DEAD; TRUMAN TO CONTINUE POLICIES; 9TH CROSSES ELBE, NEARS BERLIN

The long war had taken its toll on the president's health, and on April 12, 1945, Roosevelt suffered a stroke. He died a few hours later. Now his vice president, Harry S. Truman, became president. Truman, who was Roosevelt's third vice president, had occupied the office for only three months. He knew nothing about the Manhattan Project. Nothing! And now he had to make the decision whether to drop the bomb or not.

According to some accounts, US generals thought that Japan was "looking for peace." They told Truman there was really no military need to use the bomb. The other side of the argument was that America's use of atomic bombs would bring the war to an end sooner and save lives. Fewer people—both Japanese and Americans—would be killed from atomic bombs than from Operation Downfall.

President Truman made his decision. Drop the bomb.

Harry Truman (middle)

Harry S. Truman (1884–1972)

Harry Truman grew up poor on a farm in Missouri. He was a senator from Missouri when Roosevelt chose him to run as vice president in the 1944 election.

During his presidency (1945–1953), Truman helped create the United Nations and establish the Marshall Plan, which aimed to rebuild war-torn countries in Europe, especially Germany.

Truman often used the phrase "The buck stops here." It means that the president must make decisions and accept responsibility for those decisions. This included the decision to use the atomic bomb.

Truman always believed that dropping the bomb was the right decision.

CHAPTER 5
The Bombing of Hiroshima

At 8:16 a.m., on August 6, 1945, the first atomic bomb ever used in war exploded on Hiroshima. Within a second, the bomb's fireball was 900 feet in diameter. The blast traveled outward at 7,200 miles per hour. For miles in all

directions, metal melted. Birds burst into flames in midair. Paper 6,400 feet away (that's farther than twenty-one football fields) ignited. Glass shattered twelve miles away.

Hiroshima simply ceased to exist.

As survivor Michihiko Hachiya noted in his book, *Hiroshima Diary*, "Nothing remained except a few buildings of reinforced concrete. . . . The city was like a desert except for scattered piles of brick and roof tile. . . . I know of no word or words to describe the view."

For many hours, the Japanese government, based more than four hundred miles away in Tokyo, did not know what had happened. Communication with Hiroshima had suddenly stopped. Vague reports of some sort of large explosion began to emerge. The first real news of what happened came sixteen hours later when the United States announced the bombing.

For miles in all directions, people burned. Those closest to the explosion died instantly.

Nine out of ten people half a mile or less from ground zero were dead within minutes. (*Ground zero* means the exact point where the bomb exploded.)

Survivors recalled a blinding light and an overwhelming wave of heat. The prints on the fabrics of people's clothing were burned onto their skin. The shadows of bodies were seen on walls.

The few who survived had a hard time finding help. Nearly all doctors and nurses were killed or injured. Only three of forty-five civilian hospitals remained. Medical supplies quickly ran out. Panic set in.

As survivor Keijiro Matsushima recalled to a news source: “People were crawling towards the river, crying out for water to cool their burns. But many died on the riverbanks or drowned.”

Several days after the blast, survivors became sick from being exposed to radiation. People were vomiting and bleeding. Over the next four months, as many as 146,000 Hiroshima survivors would die of infection, blood loss, and organ failure.

Marie Curie (1867–1934)

Marie Curie was a famous scientist who studied radioactive materials. Such materials have an unstable nucleus that releases particles and energy. That release is known as radiation.

Curie is best known for the discovery of radioactive materials and for coining the word *radioactivity*.

Curie died from illness brought on by her many years of exposure to radiation.

She was the first woman to win a Nobel Prize and the only person to win in two different sciences (physics and chemistry).

But that wasn't the end of it. Health problems from radiation haunted survivors for the rest of their lives. Radiation mutates (changes) a person's cells, causing cancer. In Hiroshima, the most common type of cancer was leukemia, a blood disorder. It started appearing in survivors two years after the bombing and peaked four to six years later. For more than forty years following the bombing, its survivors were nearly twice as likely to die of leukemia than those not exposed to radiation.

The pregnant women of Hiroshima had miscarriages, stillbirths, and infancy deaths at seven times the normal rate. The babies who were born often had terrible problems.

No one will ever know for certain exactly how many died due to the bomb. The eventual death toll would exceed two hundred thousand.

Whatever Happened to the *Enola Gay*?

Following World War II, the plane was moved from place to place. Eventually, the Smithsonian Institution, in Washington, DC, took possession of the *Enola Gay*.

In 1995, the fiftieth anniversary of the end of World War II, the Smithsonian's National Air and Space Museum (NASM) proposed an exhibit.

It included a display of a restored *Enola Gay*.

In 2003, the Smithsonian opened an NASM annex near Dulles Airport. That annex now provides a permanent home for the *Enola Gay*.

Bockscar, the plane that dropped the bomb on Nagasaki, is owned by the US Air Force. It is at the National Museum of the United States Air Force at Wright-Patterson Air Force Base in Dayton, Ohio.

CHAPTER 6
Stories of Survivors

Eizo Nomura was closer to ground zero than any other survivor. He was in the basement of a building when the bomb exploded only 550 feet away. Although he survived, Nomura experienced near-fatal symptoms of radiation sickness.

In his book, *My Memories*, he recalled "Outside, it was dark because of the black smoke. It was about as light as night with a half-moon. I hurried to the foot of Motoyasu Bridge. Right in the middle and on my side of the bridge I saw a naked man lying on his back. Both arms and legs were extended toward the sky, trembling."

Sunao Tsuboi was a twenty-year-old university student on his way to school when the atomic bomb fell. His body was burned from head to toe.

Sunao was certain he would die. He told the *New York Times* that he used a small stone to scratch on a bridge, "Here is where Sunao Tsuboi found his end."

A friend rescued him from the bridge and carried him to a military hospital. Several days later, his mother and uncle found him. They took him home. It took him a year to walk again.

Sunao Tsuboi in 2015

John Hersey (1914–1993)

In spring 1946, nine months after the bombing, journalist John Hersey arrived in Hiroshima. He expected to write about the mushroom cloud, the shattered city, and the rebuilding. But instead, Hersey wrote the personal stories of just a few survivors—five Japanese and one Westerner. Through them, readers all over the world began to understand what really happened to the people of Hiroshima. His article appeared in the *New Yorker* magazine and later became a book (*Hiroshima*).

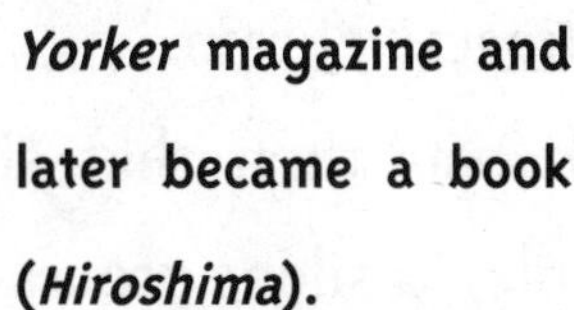

Hersey gave a voice to survivors living through a nightmare.

Later, Tsuboi fell in love and married. The couple had three children and seven grandchildren.

Keiko Ogura was eight and had stayed home from school. She was standing outside when the bomb hit. Her family's house was destroyed. Ogura shared her story with the website of the International Federation of Red Cross and Red Crescent Societies: "Thankfully my family inside the house only suffered minor injuries. Rain started to fall immediately after that . . . and my clothes were dampened by the sticky black [radioactive] rain."

It was then that she came across a line of people, "a silent procession of ghost-like figures." They were asking for water, and she gave it to them from her family's well. She did not know that water was not good for people with serious burns, and they died. She said, "I vowed never to tell anyone about what happened that day.

Keiko Ogura

My memory of that day remained with me as a nightmare even decades later."

Akiko Takakura was inside the Bank of Hiroshima, less than a thousand feet from the blast.

As noted by AtomicArchive.com, Akiko said, "I found myself in the dark. I heard my friend, Ms. Asami, crying for her mother. . . . Afraid of

being caught by a fire, I told Ms. Asami to run out of the building." They got outside but were stopped by a huge wall of fire.

Eiko Taori was in a streetcar when the bomb exploded. Holding on to her baby son, she was tossed into the street. She shared her memories with NHK, the public broadcasting company of Japan: "[My son] looked at me and smiled at my face, which was all bloody. I had plenty of milk which he drank all throughout that day." But twenty-two days later, on August 28, Taori's little son died of radiation sickness.

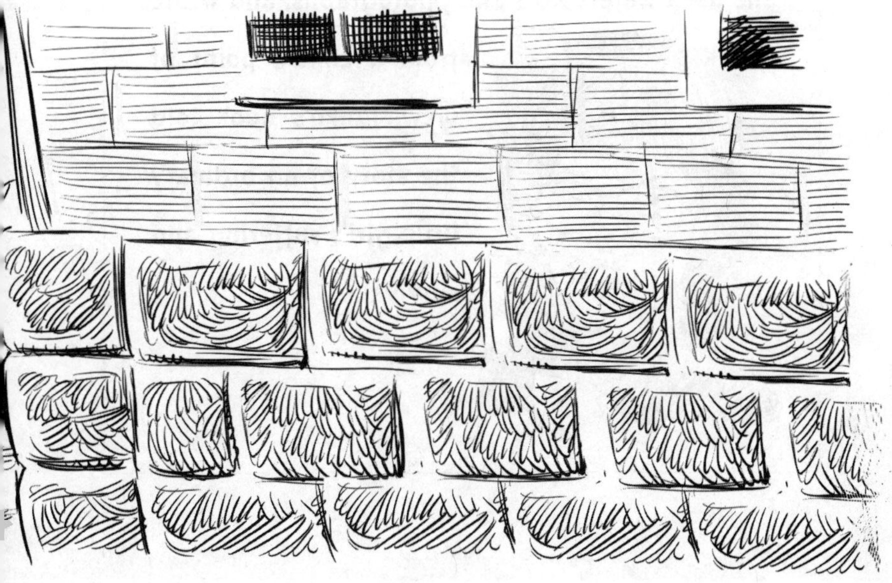

Junko Morimoto (1932–2017)

Because of a stomachache, Junko, age thirteen, was home from school when the bomb hit. Suddenly, a powerfully blinding light filled her home. A roaring sound immediately followed. Her house fell, crushing her. Junko was sure she would die. But Junko survived, becoming an award-winning author and illustrator. Forty-two years after the bombing, she published *My Hiroshima*. She wrote and illustrated her memories of that horrific day. She used watercolors and photographs, and wrote from a child's point of view. Junko's book told the story of an ordinary little girl's suffering and survival.

CHAPTER 7
The War Ends

Sixteen hours after the bombing of Hiroshima, President Truman again called for Japan's surrender. He told Japan to "expect a rain of ruin from the air, the like of which has never been seen on this earth."

Japan, however, still would not accept defeat.

So on August 9, 1945, three days after the Hiroshima bombing, the United States dropped an atomic bomb on Nagasaki, Japan. This second atom bomb was nicknamed "Fat Man."

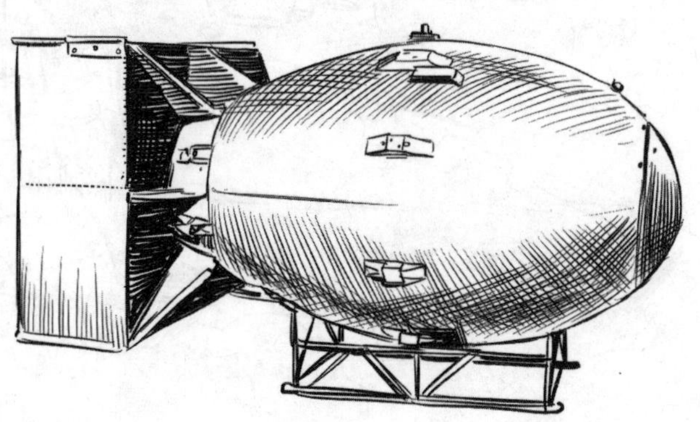

Over seventy thousand people died immediately. By the end of 1945, the total number of deaths in Nagasaki reached eighty thousand. Truman was showing Japan that the United States would continue to drop atomic bombs until Japan surrendered.

Unlike in Hiroshima, almost all of the buildings in Nagasaki were wood. As a witness

noted to the Atomic Heritage Foundation, "All the buildings I could see were on fire. . . . Electricity poles were wrapped in flame like so many pieces of kindling. . . . The sky was dark, the ground was scarlet, and in between hung clouds of yellowish smoke. . . . [People ran] about like so many ants seeking to escape. . . . It seemed like the end of the world."

A Survivor of Both Bombs

Tsutomu Yamaguchi is the only person believed to have survived both atomic bombs.

A resident of Nagasaki, he was in Hiroshima on business on August 6, 1945. The bomb's explosion ruptured his eardrums and burned much of his body. There was so much dust in the air that it made it dark as night and for a while he couldn't see.

On August 7, he somehow found a train that was still operating, and went home to Nagasaki.

Despite his wounds, Yamaguchi returned to work on August 9. A company director thought Yamaguchi's description of the bomb at Hiroshima sounded "crazy." Then suddenly they were slammed with a blinding white flash. An atomic bomb had fallen on Nagasaki.

Yamaguchi went on to live a relatively normal life. In the 2000s, he became active in the anti-atomic weapons movement. As quoted in *Military History Magazine*, he said, "The reason that I hate the atomic bomb is because of what it does to the dignity of human beings."

Yamaguchi died on January 4, 2010, at the age of ninety-three.

After the Nagasaki bombing, Japan finally agreed to the US surrender terms. On August 15, Emperor Hirohito gave a radio address to his nation. He announced Japan's surrender. On September 2, surrender papers were officially signed on the USS *Missouri* in Tokyo Bay.

World War II was over.

The Purple Heart

The United States awards a Purple Heart medal to soldiers injured or killed in battle. The Purple Heart was established in 1782 by George Washington, then head of the Continental Army.

In preparing for Operation Downfall, the United States had almost five hundred thousand Purple Hearts made. That was the number of Americans the United States expected to die in the invasion. However, Operation Downfall was scrapped in favor of dropping the bomb. That left the government with hundreds of thousands of Purple Hearts. Those Purple Hearts are still being awarded to troops today.

At the end of World War II, both Germany and Japan were occupied by their former enemies. That meant these countries were no longer in charge of themselves. They did not have a government anymore. In a defeated country, there may be no food, medicine, gasoline, or heat. Homes, office buildings, farms, and factories have been destroyed, businesses shut down. After World War II, it was up to the Allies to help both Germany and Japan rebuild as peaceful democratic nations.

Between 1945 and 1952, US general Douglas A. MacArthur led the recovery efforts in Japan. MacArthur's first job was to get food to the Japanese people. The people were starving. As one Japanese person noted, "Democracy cannot be taught to a starving people." So, the US government sent billions of dollars in food aid.

MacArthur next set out to win the support of Emperor Hirohito. Many Allied leaders wanted Hirohito put on trial as a war criminal. But MacArthur argued to do that would upset the Japanese who had suffered so much already. It was best to move on.

General Douglas A. MacArthur

Emperor Hirohito (1901–1989)

Hirohito was the emperor of Japan during World War II. The Japanese believed that the emperor was a divine descendant of a sun goddess. Unlike a president or even a king or queen, a divine ruler does not mix with citizens. Because Hirohito's voice was considered the voice of a god, the Japanese never heard him speak until he announced Japan's surrender over the radio.

Hirohito's reign began in 1926. Many of his advisers were strong military leaders. Hirohito had been taught since childhood that the emperor stayed out of politics. Instead, he should follow the advice of his advisers.

Some historians claim Hirohito was not a strong supporter of the war. They think that he was unable to stand up to the military. Others claim he took an active part in planning the war.

The Imperial Palace in Tokyo is home to the emperor and his family. The palace is surrounded by moats and massive stone walls.

When the United States bombed Japan, the emperor's palace in Tokyo was destroyed. However, Hirohito refused to leave. He wanted to go through the same hardships as his people. The palace was later rebuilt.

After the war, Hirohito was forced to say that he was not divine.

He died on January 7, 1989, Japan's longest reigning emperor. Hirohito's son Akihito became the emperor of Japan. In 1959, he broke with 1,500 years of tradition by marrying a commoner. On May 1, 2019, Akihito retired from the throne, and his son Naruhito became the new emperor.

Announcement of the new Japanese constitution

Japan now had to change in many ways. Japan was forbidden to have an army or wage war. Former military officers were barred from political leadership in the new government. In 1947, a new constitution was created. (A constitution sets up the laws and government of a country.) Elected representatives of the people would pass laws, and a prime minister—like the president in the United States—would be at the head of the government. Women in Japan got the right to vote. Labor unions were started to help workers. And poor farmers who before could only rent land could now own it.

Fukushima, 2011

Five hundred miles northeast of Hiroshima, and sixty-six years after the Hiroshima bombing, radioactive materials again poisoned Japan's air. On March 11, 2011, Japan was struck by its most powerful earthquake on record. The resulting tsunami (a giant wave) caused a nuclear power plant in Fukushima to explode and release radiation.

The Japanese government declared an "atomic power emergency." By March 13, an emergency zone extended 12.5 miles around the nuclear power plant. Over two hundred thousand people had to leave the area. As with nuclear weapons, the harmful effects of the radiation may not show for years.

Nuclear power plant explosion in Fukushima, 2011

By 1950, Japan's future looked bright. With its booming economy, Japan wanted greater independence from the United States. The United States agreed. A plan to end the occupation was begun. It allowed the United States to keep military bases in Japan. And the United States would protect Japan should it be attacked.

Japan–US relations were at last placed on a truly equal footing in 1952 when the occupation ended. Japan is now one of the world's most successful democracies.

Tokyo, present day

The United States and Japan caused each other great suffering during World War II. However, the two countries forged a strong bond after the war. To this day, they work together to keep peace in Asia and improve the lives of those in both countries.

Japanese prime minister Shinzo Abe meeting with US president Barack Obama in 2016

Three Mile Island and Chernobyl

Fukushima was not the first nuclear power accident. In 1979, an accident at the Three Mile Island nuclear power plant in Pennsylvania caused radiation to leak. Residents within a twenty-mile radius were encouraged to evacuate. Three weeks later, nearly all residents were back home. There were no known health effects.

A fatal disaster happened in 1986 at the Soviet Union's Chernobyl nuclear power plant in the Ukraine. Radioactive material was released for days. Two hundred thirty-seven people suffered radiation sickness. Thirty-one of them died within three months. Of five million people residing in its contaminated area, as many as four thousand are expected to die of a cancer caused by the accident. In the four years after the accident, nearly 350 animals on nearby farms were reported to have

been born with missing or extra limbs; missing eyes, heads, or ribs; or deformed skulls. An abandoned area known as the "zone of alienation" extends nineteen miles in all directions around the former nuclear plant. It is now a forest overrun by wildlife due to the absence of humans.

Chernobyl nuclear power plant

CHAPTER 8
What Followed

World War II was truly a world war. Nearly eighty million people around the globe were killed. And it was a war that changed what war meant. Now there were weapons that could destroy everyone on the entire planet.

After the war, the United States and the Soviet Union emerged as the world's two superpowers. And although they had been allies during the war, they were now enemies. Only four years after Hiroshima and Nagasaki, the Soviet Union tested its first nuclear bomb. That started an arms race.

The United States and the Soviet Union both rushed to build nuclear weapons. The thinking was that the nation with more weapons would be stronger and more of a threat. By the late 1960s, the United States had over thirty thousand such weapons. Missiles—ones that could be launched from silos on land or from hidden submarines—could deliver atomic bombs anywhere in the world.

The Soviet Union tests its first nuclear bomb, 1949

The threat of war was constant. By the 1950s, both the United States and the Soviet Union each had enough nuclear power to wipe out the other. Also, each side would have enough time to launch a counterattack after being attacked first. So both sides would lose. This policy was known as MAD: Mutual Assured Destruction. The hope was that knowing there could be no winner in a nuclear war would stop either superpower from attacking the other.

This period was known as the Cold War. No actual battles were fought between the two nations, but there was the constant fear that a nuclear war could start. The Cold War lasted from 1946 until the collapse of the Soviet Union in 1991.

In the United States, in the 1950s, towns prepared community-wide bomb shelters and held regular bomb drills with sirens blaring from fire stations. Many newly built houses included bomb shelters for the family.

People stocked up on canned food so that, if a nuclear war broke out, they could hide in their shelter until they believed that it was safe to emerge.

And for years, schools all across the United States held atomic bomb drills. Teachers would suddenly yell, "Drop!" Immediately, students hid under their desks with their hands over their heads. Some schools gave out metal “dog tags,” like those worn by World War II soldiers. That was done so that if anyone was killed in a nuclear attack, his or her body could be identified.

These “duck and cover” drills inspired an animated film that was sent to schools and communities. The hero of the film was Bert, a turtle who quickly ducked his head into his shell when a monkey set off a firecracker.

Of course, crawling under a small desk would provide no protection against a nuclear missile.

It was all part of the government's "emotion management" effort during the early days of the Cold War. The government felt it had to do *something* to make people feel less scared.

When not living in fear of being bombed, many Americans shrugged and found relief in being entertained by atomic-inspired films, comic books, and popular songs (like 1957's "Atom Bomb Baby"). *Them!*, a film about ants grown huge after being exposed to radiation, was one of Warner Brothers' most successful films in 1954. And the many nuclearized comic book heroes included Captain Atom and Nukla.

Yet beginning in the 1970s, US and Soviet leaders agreed to reduce the size of their nuclear arsenals. Today, the United States and Russia (which was part of the former Soviet Union) each have about 1,400 nuclear weapons ready for use. Each of those weapons is far larger than the two bombs that killed so many in Japan.

Nine countries now have nuclear weapons. Those nations are the United States, the United Kingdom, France, Russia, North Korea, Israel, Pakistan, India, and China.

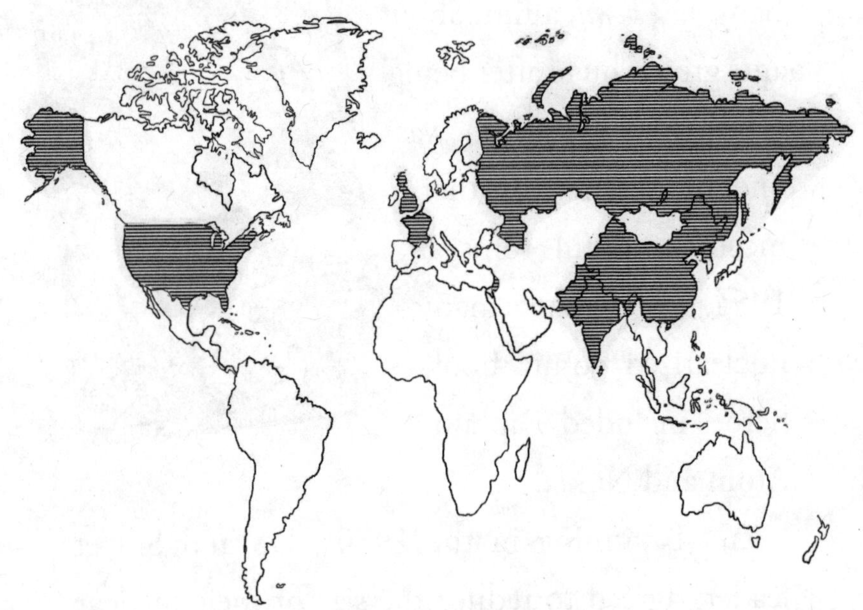

Countries with nuclear weapons, 2019

In 1968, the United States and several other nations created the Treaty on the Nuclear Non-Proliferation of Nuclear Weapons (NPT). *Non-proliferation* means preventing more countries from making nuclear weapons. Not every nuclear nation has signed the treaty, however.

Within only five years after the bombings, both Hiroshima's and Nagasaki's roads, schools, railways, hospitals, and homes were rebuilt.

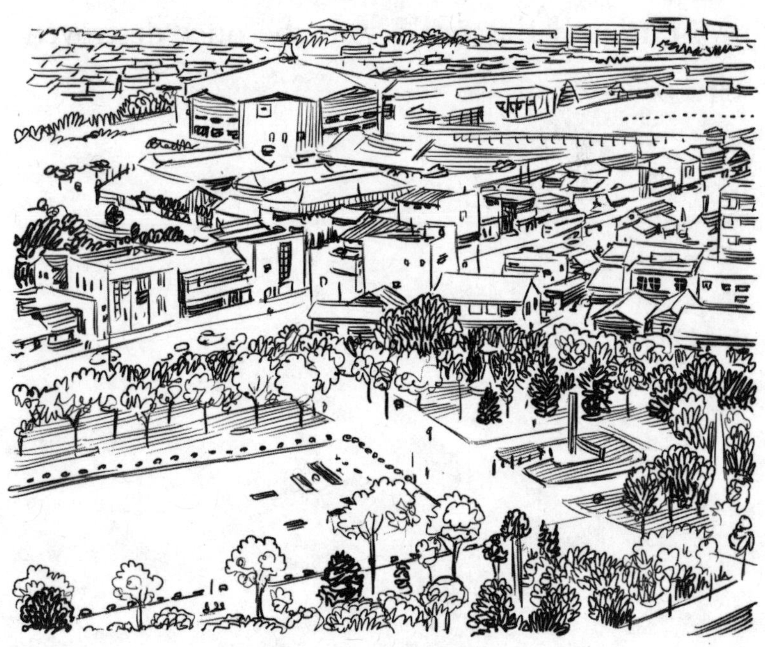

Nagasaki after it was rebuilt, 1955

Because the bombs were set off aboveground, most of the radiation cleared, leaving little in the soil. By 1955, there were more people living in each city than before they were bombed.

The cities also developed plans to bring in visitors who could honor the horrific losses while also celebrating the promise of peace. Memorials, parks, museums, and tourist facilities were built. Today, millions of Japanese people and tourists from around the world visit the once-destroyed cities every year.

CHAPTER 9
The Peace Museum

Today, Hiroshima's Peace Memorial Park is situated at ground zero. This large park of trees, lawns, and walking paths contrasts with the surrounding downtown, where all buildings were built in 1946 or after.

Before the bomb, the park was the heart of the city. It was where city government and big businesses were located. Four years later, it was decided that the area would not be redeveloped. Instead, it was devoted to peace memorials.

The park includes the Peace Memorial Museum. The museum offers a history of Hiroshima and the nuclear bomb. It welcomes

over one million visitors every year, many from other countries. Its main focus is on the dropping of the bombs and their effect. Many visitors find it to be a very difficult experience. Museumgoers are hit hard by the personal details on display. But the purpose of showing them is to help prevent another "Hiroshima" from happening.

The park also includes the A-Bomb Dome, known as the Hiroshima Peace Memorial.

A-Bomb Dome

It is what remains of the former Prefectural Industrial Promotion Hall. The hall served to promote Hiroshima's industries. When the bomb exploded, it was one of the few buildings left standing. The A-Bomb Dome stands as a link to Hiroshima's past.

Between the museum and the A-Bomb Dome is the Cenotaph for the A-Bomb Victims. (A cenotaph is a monument to people who have died, usually in war.) The cenotaph in Hiroshima honors all those whom the bomb killed. These include people who died at the initial blast, from exposure to radiation, or from later illnesses caused by the bomb. It contains a stone chest holding the names of the more than 290,000 victims.

Cenotaph for the A-Bomb Victims

Paper Cranes

Sadako Sasaki was two years old when the bomb dropped. Sadako was blown out of her family's home in Hiroshima. She was soon found with no apparent injuries. However, nine years later she became ill with leukemia. (Many in Hiroshima refer to leukemia as "atom bomb disease.")

Following the ancient Japanese craft of origami, Sadako began folding paper cranes. Japanese tradition says that if someone creates a thousand cranes, a wish will be granted. Sadako's wish was to heal and live. She folded paper cranes until her death in 1955 at age twelve.

Sadako's faith and death inspired the creation of the Children's Peace Monument. Located in Hiroshima Peace Memorial Park, it honors the memory of Sadako and all the thousands of child victims of the bomb. There, prayers are offered, including those wishing for a world without nuclear weapons.

Today, visitors to Peace Memorial Park see brightly colored paper cranes everywhere. Each year, approximately ten million paper cranes are sent in by children from across the world to the monument. They show that these children, too, hope for a world without nuclear war.

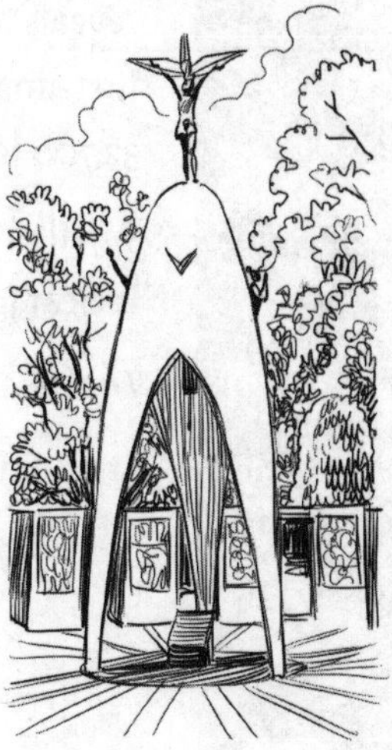

At the base of the monument is a black marble slab on which is inscribed in Japanese: "This is our cry. This is our prayer. Peace in the world."

Timeline of the Hiroshima Bombing

August 6, 1945

12:00 a.m.	Final briefing to *Enola Gay* crew; confirmation that Hiroshima remains the target
12:15 a.m.	A chaplain offers a prayer written for this occasion
1:37 a.m.	Weather planes take off to check weather conditions over the target
2:20 a.m.	Photo taken of the *Enola Gay* crew
2:45 a.m.	*Enola Gay* takes off from Tinian Island, climbs to 9,300 feet, and heads for Japan, 1,500 miles away
7:15 a.m.	Little Boy's safety devices removed and arming devices inserted
7:30 a.m.	Pilot and aircraft commander Colonel Paul Tibbets reveals to his crew, "We are carrying the world's first atomic bomb"; *Enola Gay* begins ascent to 32,700 feet; crew puts on parachutes and flak suits.
8:24 a.m.	Weather plane messages *Enola Gay* that Hiroshima is clear for bombing
9:12 a.m.	*Enola Gay* at 31,060 feet, flying 200 miles per hour
9:14 a.m.	Crew puts on protective goggles

Please Note: The* Enola Gay *took off from Tinian Island.
The times follow Tinian Island time.

9:15:15	(8:15:15 Hiroshima time) Bomb bay doors open and Little Boy is released and drops
9:16:02	(8:16:02 Hiroshima time) Bomb explodes
9:16:12	(8:16:12 Hiroshima time) Fireball is 900 feet in diameter. The blast travels outward at 7,200 miles per hour.
9:30:00	(8:30:00 Hiroshima time) Approximately 70,000 people are dead or fatally wounded
2:58 p.m.	*Enola Gay* lands back on Tinian Island

Timeline of the Making of the Atomic Bomb

1898	Marie and Pierre Curie discover polonium and radium
1933	Hungarian physicist Leo Szilard proposes a nuclear chain reaction to release energy
1938	Nuclear fission is discovered
1939	Albert Einstein warns President Franklin Roosevelt about the prospect of an atomic bomb
1940	German physicists Otto Frisch and Rudolf Peierls, working in England, propose how to construct an atomic bomb
	British prime minister Winston Churchill authorizes development of an atomic bomb
1942	Roosevelt approves production of an atomic bomb
	First modification made to B-29 bombers so they can carry atomic bombs
1944	First drop tests of dummy atomic bombs from modified B-29s in March
	First B-29s arrive in the Mariana Islands to begin a steady bombing of Japan in October

1945

- In June, the US decides to use the atomic bomb as soon as possible, on an urban area, and with no prior warning
- In July, President Harry Truman issues warning to Japan of "prompt and utter destruction" and demands Japan's surrender; Japan rejects the demand
- Hiroshima is bombed on August 6
- Nagasaki is bombed on August 9
- Japan accepts the terms of surrender on August 14
- Japan officially signs the surrender, ending World War II, in September

Timeline of World War II

1926	Hirohito becomes emperor of Japan
1933	Adolf Hitler becomes chancellor of Germany
	Franklin D. Roosevelt becomes president of the United States
	Germany's first Nazi concentration camp built
1939	Germany invades Poland, starting World War II
1940	Japanese troops invade Indochina (later called Vietnam)
1941	Japan bombs Pearl Harbor
	United States declares war on Japan and enters World War II
1942	United States launches secret program to build an atomic bomb
1943	Italy surrenders to Allied forces
1945	Germany surrenders to the Allies
	United States drops atomic bombs on Hiroshima and Nagasaki
	Japan surrenders, ending World War II
	United Nations is formed

Bibliography

***Books for young readers**

*Brallier, Jess M. ***Who Was Albert Einstein?*** New York: Penguin Workshop, 2002.

*Coerr, Eleanor. ***Sadako and the Thousand Paper Cranes***. New York: Dell, 1977.

*Demuth, Patricia Brennan. ***What Was Pearl Harbor?*** New York: Penguin Workshop, 2013.

*Frith, Margaret. ***Who Was Franklin Roosevelt?*** New York: Penguin Workshop, 2010.

Hersey, John. ***Hiroshima***. New York: Vintage; Reprint edition, 1989.

*Hillenbrand, Laura. ***Unbroken (The Young Adult Adaptation): An Olympian's Journey from Airman to Castaway to Captive***. New York: Ember, 2014.

Hogan, Michael J., ed. ***Hiroshima in History and Memory***. Cambridge: Cambridge University Press, 1996.

*Morimoto, Junko. ***My Hiroshima***. New York: Viking, 1987.

*Sheinkin, Steven. ***Bomb: The Race to Build—and Steal—the World's Most Dangerous Weapon***. New York: Flash Point, 2012.

Takaki, Ronald. ***Hiroshima: Why America Dropped the Atomic Bomb***. Boston: Little, Brown, 1995.

*Takayuki, Ishii. ***One Thousand Paper Cranes: The Story of Sadako and the Children's Peace Statue.*** New York: Laurel Leaf, 1997.

Websites

Atomic Heritage Foundation
www.atomicheritage.org

Hiroshima Peace Memorial Museum
www.hpmmuseum.jp/?lang=eng

National Archives Photo no. 434-OR-7(44)

J. Robert Oppenheimer, physicist and director of the Manhattan Project laboratory in Los Alamos

National Archives Photo no. 2002-55

US president Harry S. Truman

Emperor Hirohito of Japan

The *Enola Gay* dropped the atomic bomb on Hiroshima, 1945.

Little Boy bomb inside the *Enola Gay* plane

Mushroom cloud over Hiroshima after the bomb was dropped

National Archives Photo no. 342-AF-58189

National Archives Photo no. 243-HP-I-33-2

People walking around the ruins in Hiroshima

National Archives Photo no. 243-HP-II-210

Hiroshima in ruins after the bombing

National Archives Photo no. 243-HP-I-31-2

Few buildings in Hiroshima withstood the blast of the atomic bomb.

knowlesgallery/iStock/Getty Images Plus

The A-Bomb Dome in Hiroshima Peace Memorial Park, present day

Patricia Hamilton/Moment/Getty Images

The Cenotaph for the A-Bomb Victims in Hiroshima Peace Memorial Park

Children's Peace Monument

Malcolm P Chapman/Moment Open/Getty Images

georgeclerk/E+/Getty Images

Hiroshima today